EXPLORING SUSHANT

TRIBUTE TO THE GOOD BOY OF CINEMA

KUNAL AHER

EXPLORING SUSHANT

BY: KUNAL AHER

Contents

INTRODUCTION

Enter Caption

This book is the Tribute to the lost Gem of Cinema....Mr. Sushant Singh Rajput aka "The Good Boy of Cinema".

This Man was really really very special and way more different than other Bollywood Celebrities. He was the man with Talent, Ethics, Values, Skills and Knowledge beyond Acting, and many other great qualities that really inspired me in my life. He was also really humble ad down to earth person despite of his high achievements in life.

We'll really miss this man. So I decided to write a book on this man's life and lessons that can inspire our life too.

Never got a chance in life to meet you man. I really regret for this.

Really no words for you Sushant Sir... We really miss you. This book is a Special Tribute for

you Sir.......

- Kunal Aher

CONTENTS

ONE

THE GEM IS BORN

Sushant Singh Rajput was born on 21 January 1986 at Patna, Bihar in a middle class family. He belonged from a Rajput family. Sushant revealed in one interview that his childhood's name was Gulshan. His father Mr. Krishna Kumar Singh worked in Bihar's handloom coprporation. And his mother was a Housewife. His one of the sister Mitu Singh had also remained state level cricketer.

Sushant was the smallest family member from his family. He was an introvert child. Being a smallest member from his family he was very dear to everyone, everyone from his family loved and cared he so much that when he went outside he didn't knew how to speak and interact with people with the people. Due to all of his family member's so much of loving and caring Sushant became shy and introvert child. He was scared of stage i.e. he avoided going on stage due to lack of stage daring. Even Sushant wanted to be head boy in his school...but when he had to give the speech he, he didn't went to school on that day. He didn't wanted any attention. It's obvious that we all need some kind of acknowledgement, Sushant was getting his acknowledgement through his grades. He just had two or three close friends.

When Sushant was 16 years old, most difficult phase came in his life, his mother passed away from this world. This happened just when he gave his 12th board exams. Suddenly passing away of his mother from this world was really shocking for him because really an okay and nobody had any idea any that any such thing will happen. It was really difficult moment for Sushant but still he learnt many things from this phase where he realized how everything changes and we are just staying connected with memories. From this he started living with this philosophy that whatever is to be done should done at that time only rather than waiting for tomorrow because if we'll wait for tomorrow we'll never able to do that thing. For him his mother was the desirable women in the world for him.

His mother passed away in the year 2002 and on January he had his pre-boards, at this situation for him it was so unpredictable for him for a month (during December month) that he had failed his pre-boards almost. His mother was always worried for Sushant should take care himself and do something so that people should not say that he is not successful in his life.

Sushant have four elder sisters. He was really good in his studies since childhood because his all elder sisters were serious about studies. Physics subject was his most favorite subject. When he was in 11th standard he just loved his Physics book because he read that book for 2 years because in just 1 year he couldn't understood that book so for 2 years he kept that Physics book with him. Sushant was an avid reader. He was so brilliant to his parents joy, Class 7th he had already finished Physics and Mathematics Syllabus of Class 10th. He excelled in Board Exams and also cleared 11 Engineering Entrance Tests.

Many of the Bollywood celebrities dream to come in films since their child hood, but this was not same with Sushant. He wanted and dreamt about becoming an Air force Pilot after getting inspired from Tom Cruise's movie Top Gun. Though Sushant willed whole heartedly to become an Air force Pilot but...... his father dreamt that his child should become an Engineer thinking that it would it would open the doors for all kind of happiness for him, he'll be forever successful and forever be happy; due to which Sushant had to drop his Air force's preparation, so he dropped his Air force's preparation and started preparing for Engineering. He also had interest in Bollywood and was a huge fan Shah Rukh Khan. Sushant said that Shah Rukh Khan was great performer but that didn't impacted him most; indeed Sushant said that Shah Rukh Khan helped him to sort out his confusion for who he (Sushant) should be.

It was 90's and the economy was just opening up, many international brands were brands were coming in, Sushant was fascinated by them...but yet confused for whether to embrace West culture or be honest and loyal to Indian culture. During this time when Sushant was in 6th Standard SRK's movie called "Dilwale Dulhania

Le Jayenge" was released; Sushant told that in that movie it the character Raj showed him that it was cool to have a beer, but Raj also waited for Simran's dad's approval...there was a balance. Sushant said that in that movie it was the perfect marriage of an aspiring India and an India trying to hold on its culture.

He said once "Engineering wasn't my choice. I wanted to be an astronaut, and later, an Air Force pilot. I remember tearing up my Top Gun poster when my parents told me that was not going to happen. Apparently, I was going to be an engineer. Maybe the drama I did that day should've given everyone a clue! But truly, I was gutted......In a family of doctors and lawyers, I guess there was little room for anything else. My three elder sisters and a brother were all great in academics, and so the expectation was already set high. Not doing well was not an option. As you can imagine, being an actor was not even on the horizon."

Sushant was also interested in Engineering so he gave an Entrance Exam for Delhi Engineering College. Now being an intelligent guy and incredible in studies Sushant secured 7th Rank in AIEEE (All India Entrance Exams) in 2003 and really a very big achievement. Sushant was really a brilliant student as he had won several National Olympiad in Physics.

Everyone needs money for his or her own purpose. When Sushant was in First Year in Delhi College he used to teach to the aspiring Engineering students for earning money. From his own earnings he bought his first bike.

Now many of us being an engineering or college students have a little bit of attraction for beautiful girls, maybe we dream to fall in relationships at his stage to make our college life more interesting; Sushant was a Mechanical Engineering Student but there was not even a single girl in his class due to which he started to feel his college life too boring. During his speech which in IIT Bombay he said "UPSC exams were still far away. In the meantime, I thought of doing theatre and I thought to learn dance because to counter the shyness that I had, still have, and also because there were no girls in my engineering college for some reason. I felt cheated man, we slogged so much, you cracked your entrance exam, and you find that there are no girls. So yeah. So, somebody told me that there are very good-looking girls in dance schools. So, I was like, fine, I enrolled."

He also said once "There were hardly any girls around! Here I was, thinking I will finally meet some nice girls when I go to college, but it turns out not too many girls take up engineering, or did, back in the day when I joined Delhi College of Engineering..."

Talking about Sushant's first love in one of the interview he said that his first love was in his 4th standard because his teacher "was very nice". In his school days being a shy and introvert gut he never dared to "PROPOSE" any girl. He got his first proposal in his 9th standard he said jokingly in that interview it took 5 years for predation for his first love proposal i.e. from 4th Standard to 9th Standard.

Sushant always had the habit of dreaming big. This man never settled for something average......

TWO

Swapping from Engineering to Dance & Acting

Sushant was brilliant in his studies. He had cleared several Engineering Entrance exams through his hard work and dedication. So there was the celebration in his family too. He was telling himself that "you what, now you have made it. You should be happy because you're supposed to be happy..." but it wasn't working as expected. He felt that something was missing, he felt that something was lacking in his life. He thought may be something bigger was required. He felt future for him was much happier, much happier than the present moment for him. So it was like, fine for him, it was just like he was forcing himself. So he started preparing for civil services examination and he was forcing himself to strive to work hard....but he was bored.

UPSC Exams were still far away. He thought of doing theatre and also thought of doing theatre....to reduce shyness which he had...he said which he still have. One more reason behind this was there were no girls present in his engineering college due to some reason. As we know he felt cheated for working hard to crack the

Entrance exams and no girls present in the college. Somebody told Sushant that there very good-looking girls in dance schools. So it was fine for him, he enrolled for the dance classes.

He started performing arts. And once he started performing arts, he knew one thing for sure, that he quite likes his work. He realized that he was really interested in arts. He wanted to earn money and to recognize.

It was 2006, Sushant's final year college, when he dropped out from the college. When his family heard that Sushant had dropped out from the college it was like a bomb for him. They were shocked! So shocked that they couldn't say anything....Sushant took their silence as his approval. It was really hard situation for him at this time. But afterwards it was different for his parents...his dad was really proed for his achievements..But still yet his father used to say to him "beta, degree le leta..."

When Sushant was preparing for his Engineering Entrance exams; he'd sometimes take a break and stand in front of a mirror and lip-sync to 'Suraj Hua Maddham'. He used to do these things nut not with the ambition of becoming actor but just for

fun. Sushant once said if anyone would have offered him a role back at that time he would have refused because he was complete introvert.

Sushant dropped out from the college when he was just two semesters from getting

the degree...the ENGINEERING DEGREE.

Sushant came to Mumbai. He started working so hard and with dedication and striving to in learning the skills that he thought were necessary to become an actor. By this time he stayed with six other fellows in a single room kitchen. But this time....Sushant was prepared for the struggle which had to face for achieving something in his life. He was driven. His self-respect was at risk. Many of the Sushant's ex-classmates thought that he was a kind of disaster that people in engineering and should never become. So he had to prove a point to everybody, he had to prove his family and he had to prove a point himself that he can be what he wanted in his life and willed.

This was the time when Sushant had also became a background dancer. He was dancing behind all the stars like Shah Rukh Khan, Shaheed Kapoor, Hritk Roshan etc. He used think himself while performing.. He used to say "okay, it's just three steps away, there I have to get, and everything will be sorted. And just after two years later Sushant was selected for a prime time show on a TV. It was re ally a big break for him he had started earning and even started getting recognized by the people. He used to deliberately go and roam in all these malls so that people would smile at him and ask for photograph.

No one from from Sushant's family knew that he used to spend more time in dance classes rather than his college. His father came to know about this when Sushant had to go Australia and he didn't had passport. For making passport sushant told his father everything and looking towards his passion for dance his father supported him.

Sushant was watching himself on TV for the first time. It was really an exhilarating moment for him and he was looking at himself everyday on TV. He was making a good money at this point that money had stopped being a differentiator in my life and he was becoming more and more popular.

Sushant may have gone to dancing classes in search of girls but he really liked dance. He got selected for for Shiamk Davr's 'special potentials' batch. One day Shiamk Davar asked Sushant "You are not one of my best dancers but there is something about the way you express that makes me pick you for my first row...why don't you try theatre?"

He had never thought about this. By taking Shiamk Davr's advice Sushant joined Barry John's acting class.In his Acting class while everybody got C he got B Grade at the end of his three month Diploma Course. From he started taking acting seriously as a potential career. He started reading everything related to acting including Stanislavski. The Grades at Barry's assured him that he can trained as an actor and by this time he also started enjoying on stage. After previous year of being shy, he could now say and do things that he wanted to. The stage unleashed him, liberated him. He could engage the audience; people were getting connected to Sushant for what he was doing on stage. He could make the audience laugh and cry.

Sushant had brought his first dream house for him. He brought his first dream car for him. And most importantly he was getting such a female attention that any of his engineering college friends could hardly dream of.

But then something unusual happened, Sushant got used to everything and he felt cheated. He stayed with all these dreams for 10 and 15 years of his life. He was promised happiness and success. But unfortunately these things stayed with him just for few days. He was interrupting himself for several times for he had started from zero money and zero recognition. Due to which he was not happy. Sushant didn't liked his this version of success. So this time he decided, he would do something else.

Now many would call the years before Sushant had hit the Bollywood the struggling period. But for him he was not struggling. He was already doing what he loved. He was doing theatre, going for castings, training in marital arts, working as background dancer, watching and discussing films with his roommates who were also actors.

In between he had to cook; they just had one pressure cooker and dal, chawal, vegetables, all would go in it together. He would cook his dishes and laundry and other household chores, which were really exhausting for him but still did it because he took this all as a part of a game.

THREE

Entering in TV Serials and Films

After joining the dance classes Sushant also started getting interest in Theatres. Here his acting journey started. He did theatre for few years. While he was doing theatre Sushant was spotted by Balaji Telefilms while he was working at Prithvi Theatre.

He was afterwards called for an audition and got cast as a secondlead in the television series called 'Kis Desh Mein Hai Meera Dil'. In this TV Serial he got the role of Preet Singh Juneja, who was the step brother of lead character named Harshad Chopda and entered the show in this serial's seventh episode. Now while this TV Serial was going on the character of Sushant was killed early in the show....but due to the popularity gained by this character among the viewers it was brought back in the series final as spirit looking on as his family celebrated coming out of difficult times. Sushant's performance was so brilliant and tremendously amazing that it made an impression on the producer Ekta Kapoor. Ekta Kapoor

confirmed him to be the playing the lead cast role in another TV Serial 'Pavitra Rishta'.

Sushant was cast as Manav Deshmukh who was an 'ideal son and husband' in this serial and co-starred with Ankita Lokhande. This role of Manav Deshmukh was really a breakthrough for Sushant and for which he had also won several awards. He won his first for best actor in Indian Television Academy Awards in 2010.

Being an actor in 2010 Sushant also joined the dance reality show called "Zara Nachke Dikha" in its second season as part of the "Mast Kalandar Boys" team. On Mother's Day special episode of this show, the team dedicated a performance to Sushant's mother who had left this world. Later in the same year, he also took part in fourth season for another dance reality show called "Jhalak Dikhla Ja" paired alongside with the choreographer Shapma Sonthalia; this dance pair emerged as the runner-ups of the season.

Sushant worked in 'Pavitra Rishta' for almost 2 years and at that time he was the most in demanding actors in TV industry. Various TV Serials were planned for Sushant i.e. he had several offers. But he felt monotonous in just acting in TV

Serials and being an actor he was not growing in an entertainment industry. So decided to leave the TV Serials and enter in the film industry.

Sushant knew one thing that TV actors get very less success in the Bollywood industry...but despite of this he took risk for this. He was so confident on this his decision that before signing his first film he had been 5 films which he rejected.

Sushant also decided that he'll go to USA and will do the filmmaking course for which he took admission in University of California, Los Angeles. Many of the Hollywood's renowned personalities have been studied in this university. Sushant was really good exposure here. But just like he was not able to complete his engineering degree similarly he was also not able to complete his filmmaking course because he had been offered the role of Ishaan Bhatt, a district-level cricketer who was a victim of politics, he was one of the leads along with Rajkummar Rao and Amit Sadh for the film 'Kai Po Che'. He thought that this role was perfect for him for his debut film. Hardly three to four months were remaining for Sushant to complete his filmmaking course but for 'Kai Po Che' he took the risk of leaving that course.

Film 'Kai Po Che' was successful on box office and people appreciated all three actors but Sushant gained most of the popularity from this film after which Yash Raj Films signed fim for another film 'Shudh Desi Romance'.

Sushant also got his first commercial advertisement for Pepsi in 2013. He got this advertisement after his success in the film 'Kai Po Che'.

Bollywood's every actor dreams to work with Raj Kumar Hirani. SUshant got his opportunity in his third film 'PK' in which he played the role of Sarfraz which was cameo appearance. For playing this role he didn't charged any fees because just wanted to work with Raj Kumar Hirani due to which he didn't kept any demand for money.

In 2011, a biopic on the life of Mahendra Singh Dhoni ny Dhoni's manager Arun Pandey. This project had to face several difficulties like objections from the Board of Control for Cricket in India (BCCI) including Dhoni's demand for a large royalty. On 25th September 2014, Sushant was announced as an actor who would play the role of Dhoni in the biopic titled as 'M.S. The Untold Story' which was directed by Neeraj Pandey.

The way Sushant mastered the character of Mahendra Singh Dhoni was really incredible and probably wouldn't have been possible for any other actor. Before this film Sushant was not even to play the cricket properly but he was the big fan of MS Dhoni. For Dhoni's character he prepared himself for about one and half years in which he mastered Dhoni's cricketing style and even small-small gestures of Dhoni. But understanding MS Dhoni's mindset was the most tuff work for Sushant. Sushant said that "by training I can play cricket like Dhoni and even changing looks I can look like, but thinking like Dhoni was really a difficult job for me." When Sushant used to meet Dhoni he always used to ask several questions to him due to which Dhoni used to get irritate to him. Once Sushant carried a paper of 250 MCQs questions and after seeing this Dhoni was completely shocked. Dhoni used to tell him "you ask lot of questions man... Wait I'll just be back in two minutes..."

Talking about his another film 'Detective Byomkesh Bakshy!' The story of this film was based on 1940's era. For playing the role in this movie just like 'MS Dhoni: The Untold Story' in this movie too he did trained himself hard. As we know in 1940's there no such mobile technology present at that time so Sushant also stopped using the mobile phone. It four months for shooting of this film and for four months Sushant didn't used his mobile phone. Even he stopped driving his car for because the character of Detective Byomkesh Bakshy is seen to be walking or using any other public transport. So for this Sushant avoided several of his luxurious things so that he can understand his character in a better way.

Sushant used to think that in his career he had not played any glamorous character which he can show to his father. His father used to think that the hero who fights, kicks, punches the villain. But Sushant didn't had any such film. So when his film 'Raabta' was released he showed this film to his father because in this film he did several action scenes. In one of the interview Sushant said that his father loved his film 'Raabta' so much and watching the film he even Sushant to do more such films.

In film 'Raabta' he had to do several fight scenes, he had to fight with two swords at a time for which he took training for several months. He was an actor who mostly used the technique called 'Method Acting' in his career.

In film 'Kedarnath' we see Sushant in the role of Mansoor Khan whose work was to carry the people on his back and take them to Kedarnath. It's really difficult to carry someone on your back and walk but Sushant did all these scenes by himself. Film's director Abhishek Kapoor said that physically for anyone these scenes are really difficult and when told to retake such kind of scene actors really feel upset and annoyed for this...but Sushant never created any issue for this and he always supported his team for retakes. If he wanted he would have body double roles for such scenes but he was not that kind of actor, his method of acting was such that loved to feel his every character, so if you watch any of his film his hard work and dedication is clearly shown in his films.

Like Sushant gave big hits in movies. Simlarly just like other up and downs, Sushant's career's big flop was 'Sonchiriya'. Though this movie was flop but the performance of Sushant was really amazing in this movie.

In 2019, film 'Chhichhore' which was directed by Nitesh Tiwari, in this movie Sushant played the role of Anirudh Pathak. Sushant had a personal reason for signing this film. When Sushant came to know that this film's most of the part will shot in college so for this reason he signed this film. Before this film Sushant hadn't did any college film and he really wished to this kind of film.

Sushant's last film of his life is Dil Bechara...

No matter Sushant had few flops on box office but Sushant's dedication was showed across the different roles he played. He was the man who took craft of acting very seriously.

FOUR

Sushant's Speeches on his Life

Following are the speeches given by Sushant which are really inspiring. In the following speeches he is talking about his life journey. There 2 speeches which I've included, each speech with life journey but different learnings from these 2 speeches. These speeches given by Sushant will surely inspire us for leading our lives towards the big achievements.

1. **Sushant's 2006 speech given in IIT Bombay:**

"I had this habit of carrying chits in colleges.

Well, before we get going, I have a confession to make. I became an actor because I had a problem. I was an introvert. You know, I'm the youngest in my family. And I was so pampered in my house that when I used to step out, I didn't know how to deal with people. So, I gradually became this very shy, introverted kid who could not talk. Well, I still cannot talk. And I have stage fright. So, in case, so what I do generally as an actor is I hide behind all these fascinating characters, and then I'm confident. But, like right now as I'm not acting, so... I will screw it up. So, excuse me if I falter. Excuse me if I don't make sense. Excuse me if I get a panic attack right now. But I will try my best.

We love you anyway.

Alright. I would love to share my journey with you, my learnings, and in case you decide to drop out and join me in Bollywood, it will come very handy. So, I was thinking in the car, what do I talk about? What can I tell you that you already don't know? I'm assuming, and I think most probably, you guys are way much smarter and better than what

I was when I was your age. You know, you already know about the cut-throat competition, you know the importance of hard work, perseverance, and vision, focus, self-belief, etc., etc. So, I don't need to talk about that.

But after deep thinking, I zeroed down into two things that I can actually discuss about. These two things talk about chasing your dreams and actually living your dreams, which unfortunately nobody mentioned to me when I was starting out.

And those two things are, can I write them, can you see enough words? Alright, so yeah, so those two things are the biggest lie and the only truth about success that I was told about.

Now the biggest lie was money plus recognition is equal to happiness, is equal to success. So, let me begin by mentioning that I come from a very middle-class family. And when I was growing up, money was a big, big, big differentiator in my life. Also, in the three generations of my family that I know of, that are documented, nobody knew what fame felt like. So, basically, both money and recognition were missing when I started out. So, I already started out as a failure, let me be very precise.

My family told me that I had to become an engineer, medicals were booked for my sisters. So, once I'm an engineer, then I can, you know, try civil services examination and then probably, yeah, that would be like opening the doors for all kinds of happiness and I'll be forever successful, I'll be forever happy. This is the condition that I experienced when I was growing up. Alright, fair enough, good deal.

So, I became very good in studies, did fairly well in my 10th board exams, and then off I went to Delhi for my +2, got myself enrolled in a nice school and Vidya Mandir and FIIT JEE and half a dozen of another coaching institutes. And I used to share my room with three other similar aspirants. What it meant was every day after finishing my assignments, school assignments, and preparing for my engineering entrance exam, I had to wash my clothes and I had to cook food for myself. But I wasn't complaining. Well, it was worth it because after all, I was for the very first time in my life, I was so close to become successful, for the first time in my life. So yeah, finally I slopped, I got selected for several engineering colleges and I decided to take admission in Delhi College of Engineering, whichis...

DC.

Now known as DTU, thank you. Were you my senior or junior?

So, yeah, so there was a celebration like this in my family too. I could finally stop for a while and breathe, you know. I was telling myself that, you know what, now you have made it. You should be happy because you're supposed to be happy, but it wasn't working that much. Something was missing, there was a void that I could feel. So, I thought maybe something bigger was required. For some reason, incessantly while the first 18, 19 years of my life, the future me was much happier, much successful than the present me. So, I was like, alright fine, so I was forcing myself. As I promised, I started preparing for civil services examination and I was forcing myself to slog, but I was bored.

UPSC exams were still far away. In the meantime, I thought of doing theatre and I thought to learn dance because to counter the shyness that I had, still have, and also because there were no girls in my engineering college for some reason. I felt cheated man, we slogged so much, you cracked your entrance exam, and you find that there are no girls. So yeah. So, somebody told me that there are very good- looking girls in dance schools. So, I was like, fine, I enrolled.

And once I started with performing arts, I knew one thing for sure, I knew that I quite liked it. And three years later, imagine me sitting in the campus and I'm thinking, alright, I'm really interested in performing arts. And all I want to do is to earn money and to be recognized. So, if I become a movie star, hmm, I actually was very serious. And I dropped out of my College in the third year, when I was just two semesters away from getting the degree, engineering degree.

Came to Mumbai, got heavily into theatre and also the skills that I thought were necessary to become an actor. And by the way, this time I stayed with six other guys in a single room kitchen. But this time I was prepared for it. This time, there was one difference, I was driven. My self-respect was at stake. My ex-college mates, one of them is sitting right here in the black shirt. They thought that I was that disaster that folks in engineering and B schools should never become. So, I had to prove a point to everybody. I had to prove a point to my family. Most importantly, I had to prove a point to myself.

And this was the time when I was also a background dancer. So, I was dancing behind all the possible stars that you can think of, Shahrukh Khan, Shaheed Kapoor, everybody. And I was thinking, I was thinking to myself while I was performing, okay, it's just three steps away, there I have to get, and everything will be sorted. And I kept going like that. And two years later, guess what, I got myself my first big break. I was selected for a prime time show on TV.

Now hear me out. It was seriously a big break because I started earning, people started recognizing me. To be honest, I would deliberately go and roam in all these malls so that people could look at me, smile, ask for my photograph.

And I was watching myself on TV for the first time. You have no idea how it feels for somebody like me to, you know, just looking at me for, and I was looking at myself every day on TV. It was a big, big, big high. I also suddenly discovered that I actually had many friends, who were absent all this while, but suddenly they popped up. And the show became popular. I was making good money to a point that money stopped being a differentiator in my life. And I was becoming more and more popular. Now I cannot go to all these malls that I was going all alone. So, I wanted somebody to be with me, to save me.

So, you know what I'm saying? I bought myself my first dream house. I bought myself my dream car. And just a note, to you as well, I was getting such female attention that my engineering college friends could only possibly dream of.

So, I was having a time of my life. And then something unusual happened, I got used to everything and I felt cheated. I stayed with all these dreams for 10 and 15 years of my life. I was promised happiness and I was promised success. But all these things stayed with me just for a few days. And I'm punctuating me because I started from zero money and zero recognition. So, I was not happy. How could that it be? I didn't like this version of success. And the future me, again, was hearing the present me. But this time, I decided otherwise, I would do something else.

So, that gets us to the second point, which is the only truth, I won't take too much time, I will just try to keep it short. I figured something, I figured that something, seemingly big things, were not that big once I got them. And looking back in the past, I realized that maybe smaller things were way bigger. And there was one thing that was missing in my life that was the cause of this illusion. And that thing that was missing was NOW. I was all of these years, just I was obsessed about what's going to happen. I used to draw those flow charts that we're taught in schools. If this happens, I'll do that. And six months from now, I'll be here. So, I want it to be in control. I was so obsessed about my future, I was taking the entire responsibility about the past, but all I was doing was frequently swinging from past to future, not living in actual sense.

Well, I also figured that when I perform on stage or in front of the camera, I'm so much excited. I am so much interested. I was paying so much attention that there was no room to think about the future or the past. I was just there in the moment; I was alive in true sense when I was performing. And for the first time, trust me, in a long time, I understood the true meaning of success, which was not money plus recognition, but it was NOW plus excitement.

So, here I am right now, five years down the line, money, and fame although still could not earn back their reputation in my life. But let me show you one thing, I have much more of them than I had ever planned. And the best thing, my college, one of the professors was very dear to me, called me recently about asking me to plan this interaction with students. And I very humbly requested that can I get my degree back.

And it's happening. And I'm very excited, again. Thank you so much, guys."

1. **Speech 2:**

"The college compound was huge, just as Bollywood movies promise you. I was a wide-eyed boy from Patna in Delhi, befitting the typical hero. It was the first day of college. The stage was set for me to bump into the heroine. But where was she?

There were hardly any girls around! Here I was, thinking I will finally meet some nice girls when I go to college, but it turns out not too many girls take up engineering, or did, back in the day when I joined Delhi College of Engineering...

Engineering wasn't my choice. I wanted to be an astronaut, and later, an Air Force pilot. I remember tearing up my Top Gun poster when my parents told me that was not going to happen. Apparently, I was going to be an engineer. Maybe the drama I did that day should've given everyone a clue! But truly, I was gutted.

In a family of doctors and lawyers, I guess there was little room for anything else. My three elder sisters and a brother were all great in academics, and so the expectation was already set high. Not doing well was not an option. As you can imagine, being an actor was not even on the horizon.

It wasn't like I was unaffected by Bollywood, no. I was a huge fan of Shah Rukh Khan. I remember watching *Dilwale Dulhania Le Jayenge* (*DDLJ*) and thinking now here's a cool dude. He is a great performer, but that's not what impacted me most: Shah Rukh helped me sort out my confusion about who I should be. This was in the early '90s and the economy was just opening up – we were seeing Coke cans for the first time, international brands were coming in, and I was fascinated...yet confused. I didn't know whether to embrace the West or be loyal to our culture. At this point came *DDLJ*, I was in Class VI, and Raj showed me that it was cool to have a beer, but then he also waited for Simran's dad's approval. There was a balance. It was the perfect marriage of an aspiring India and an India trying to hold on to its culture.

Shah Rukh helped me sort out my confusion about who I should be. This was in the early '90s and the economy was just opening up...I was fascinated, yet confused. I didn't know whether to embrace the West or be loyal to our culture. At this point came DDLJ Raj showed me that it was cool to have a beer, but then he also waited for Simran's dad's approval. There was a balance.

I was good at studies. To my parent's great joy, in Class VII, I'd already finished the Physics and Math syllabus of Class X. I excelled in the board exams, cleared 11 engineering entrance tests, won the National Olympiad in Physics and landed in the Delhi College of Engineering.

So here I was, and here were the lack of girls. After being a nerd so far, I was hoping to change my luck in college but that looked doubtful now. Then, one day a friend suggested that if I really wanted to meet girls, I should join dancing classes. Apparently all the cool girls of Delhi were into dancing at that time. I was doing well in my course so I could afford to take the time out. This was the key turning point of my life...

I'd sometimes take a break and stand in front of the mirror and lip-sync to Suraj Hua Maddham. (Suit from Canali, shirt from Brooks Brothers and shoes from Bally) (Subi Samuel)

Honestly, even if I would've been offered a role back then, I would've refused because I was a complete introvert. The lip-syncing and posing would happen only in front of the mirror, with just me in the audience.

Thinking back, I now see that the tell-tale signs were always there. While preparing for engineering entrance exams, I'd sometimes take a break and stand in front of the mirror and lip-sync to *Suraj Hua Maddham*. I used to do these things but not with the ambition of becoming an actor. It was just for fun. Honestly, even if I would've been offered a role back then, I would've refused because I was a complete introvert. The lip-syncing and posing would happen only in front of the mirror, with just me in the audience. I wanted to be the head boy in my school but, when I had to give a speech, I didn't go to school that day. I didn't want any attention. Of course, we all need some kind of acknowledgement, but I was getting that with my grades. I had just two or three close friends but that was it. Life was perfect! Or so I thought.

Many would call the years before I hit Bollywood the struggling period but not me. I was not struggling. I was already doing what I loved. (Suit by Selected Homme, shirt by Canali and shoes from O'keeffe) (Subi Samuel)

Then, I felt the need to meet a girl, and that led me to Shiamak Davar's group. My life went into a spin from that point on. Instead of heading to Stanford University from where I had a scholarship offer, I dropped out of college and landed in Versova, in a 1RK (room kitchen) that I shared with six others. You can imagine the reaction at home.

t was 2006, my final year in college, when I dropped this bomb at home. They were shocked! So shocked that they couldn't say anything and I took their silence as their approval!

It was 2006, my final year in college, when I dropped this bomb at home. They were shocked! So shocked that they couldn't say anything and I took their silence as their approval.... It was hard at that time but now it's different. My dad loves it when, on his walks, people call out to him, show him some recent clipping on me...he is really proud of me. But even today, almost all our conversations end with "beta, degree le leta..."

The stage unleashed me, liberated me. (Sushant wears a suit, shirt and pocket square from Brooks Brothers and shoes from O'Keeffe) (Subi Samuel)

I may have gone to dancing classes looking for girls but I really liked it! I got selected for Shiamak's 'special potentials' batch. One day he said: "You are not one of my best dancers but there is something about the way you express that makes me pick you for my first row...why don't you try theatre?"

After all these years of being shy, I could now say and do things I wanted to, behind the garb of the character. The stage unleashed me, liberated me.

I had never thought about it. But taking his advice, I joined Barry John's acting class and, to my surprise, while everyone else got a C, I got a B at the end of that three-month diploma course. This is when I started seriously thinking of acting as a potential career. My nerd instinct kicked in and I started reading up everything I could find on acting, including Stanislavski. The grades at Barry's assured me that I can be trained as an actor and by this time I had also started enjoying being on stage. After all these years of being shy, I could now say and do things I wanted to, behind the garb of the character. The stage unleashed me, liberated me. I could engage the audience; the people were connecting with what I was doing on stage. I could make them laugh or cry. For the first 20 years of my life, it was difficult to get people to understand me, but now I could do it easily. That gave me a real high.

I am not here for money or fame, I am here because I love to act (Subi Samuel).

Many would call the years before I hit Bollywood the struggling period but not me. I was not struggling. I was already doing what I loved! I was doing theatre, going for castings, training in martial arts, working as a background dancer, watching and discussing films with my roomies who were also actors. Yes, in between, I'd have to cook (we just had one pressure cooker and dal, chawal, vegetables, all would go in it together), do my dishes and laundry and other household chores, which were exhausting, but I took it all as part of the game. Even today, when I have money, fame, films, I have the same level of excitement for my job that I had back then. My career is not an upward graph from theatre to television to movies; I was and am equally excited about what I am doing at the moment.

It is important that the role excites me. While reading the script, I like to find my way to play the character. If I already know how to go about with the character, for me the charm is lost.

Being a trained dancer and a martial arts performer, it would've been easier for me to do an action film or some dance numbers. Those movies make money but that's not my interest. I am not here for money or fame, I am here because I love to act. It is important that the role excites me. While reading the script, I like to find my way to play the character. If I already know how to go about with the character, for me the charm is lost.

Even if I play a complex part to perfection, the film might not work at the box office. That does not affect me. For one Friday I can't put my life on hold – either to celebrate or to sulk. Friday depends on the audience and the critics, but the Monday is mine to decide the course of the week!

I'm not saying success is not important. It changes things; mostly people's perception of you. After *Detective Byomkesh Bakshy!* (2015), media found me to be honest and endearing. The same people found me arrogant after the success of the Dhoni biopic. I understand sensationalism sells – if Sushant was nice and humble before, and he is the same now then there is no news! I will not claim that these things don't affect me. In fact, I want to be affected by these. I want some vulnerability to remain; that's what makes me human."

- Inspiring Speeches by Mr. Sushant Singh Rajput. Thanks Sushant for your inspiring lines of your journey.

FIVE

BEYOND ACTING

Sushant was no doubt was a very talented actor. His dedication was seen in his each and every movie.

But Sushant was not just only a talented actor and dancer he was beyond that. He had several interests beyond films and entertainment industry.

When in the world of glamour many stars when talk about something they appear to be self-obsessed and very shallow. It seems that rather than the film industry and filmy world they don't know anything what's happening around the world.

But Sushant was very very special. He genuinely loved science. Even though he had achieved greater success in his life, he never forget his love for his favorite subject Physics.

Once a Cambridge PhD scholar student named Dr. Namrata Patta met Sushant by chance. She took Sushant as a Physicist. The two ended up talking for about two hours. "We had hours to kill before our flight. I sat down with a beer n he politely asked if he could join me. Then we got into talking, and a lot of it. He is such a delightful person," Namrata recalled. "I had no idea he was a Bollywood star. I thought he was a physicist studying in France. The way he was explaining physics was mesmerising. Later he told me he is an actor and I actually asked him Why?" she said. Namrata said that actor was very much interested in learning and discovering new things. She wrote, "He asked me about my thesis n won't stop until I explained the methodology involved. He paid attention to every word I said n would question until he understood them. His enthusiasm is what kept us going on talking for 5 whole hours." She also told ""The way he explained quantum physics to me at Paris airport, I knew I was talking to a genius." To keep their both conversation going, she asked Sushant ""What is the one thing you would want to change?" Sushant told her that he wanted to study physics. He also asked her whether if could apply for scholarships to get into physics. Here's her tweet.....

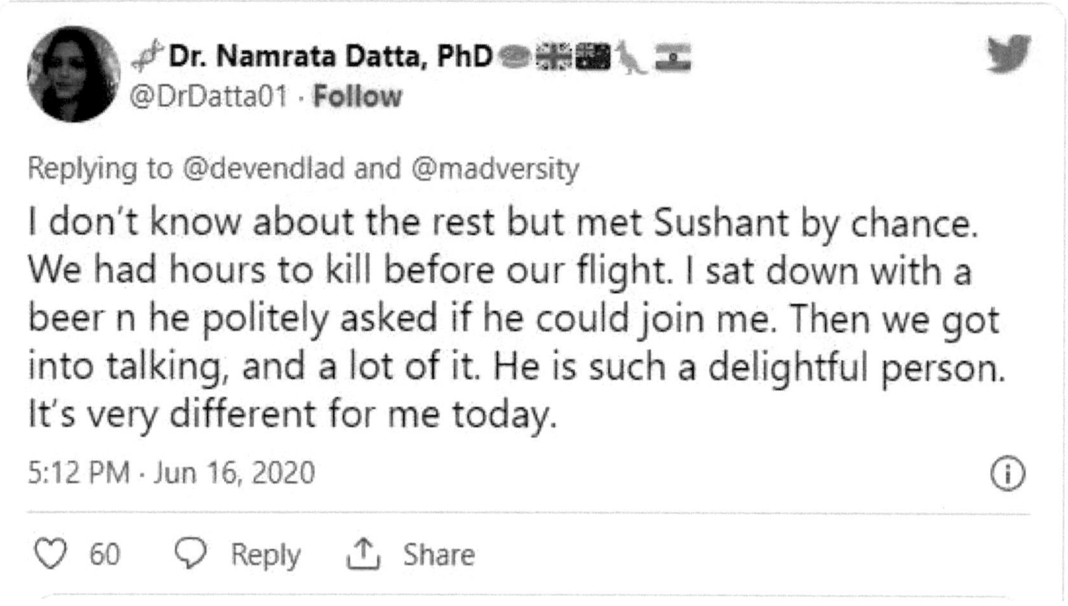

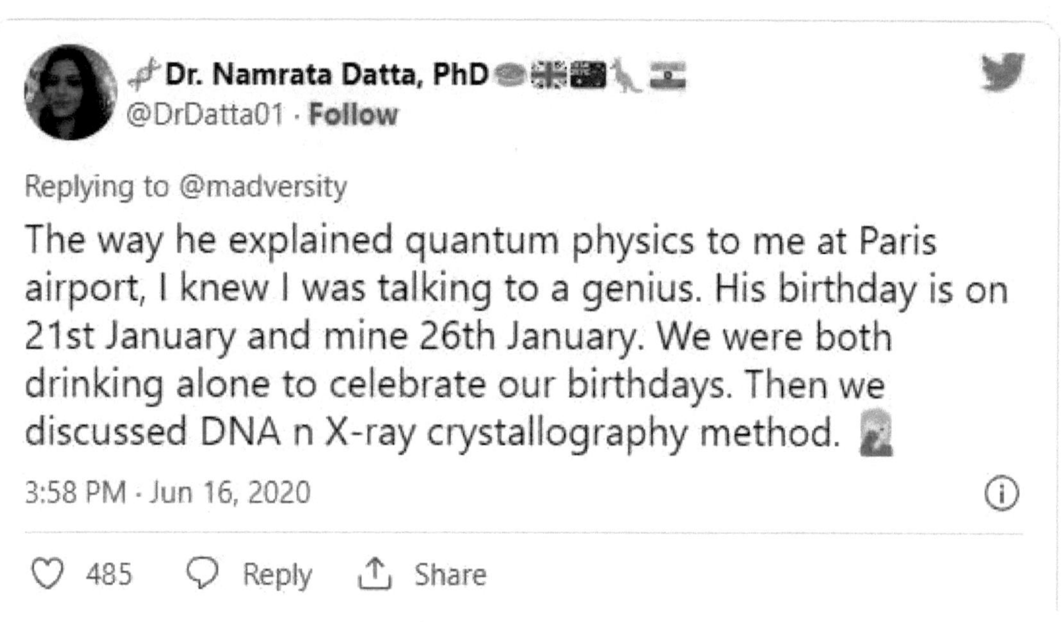

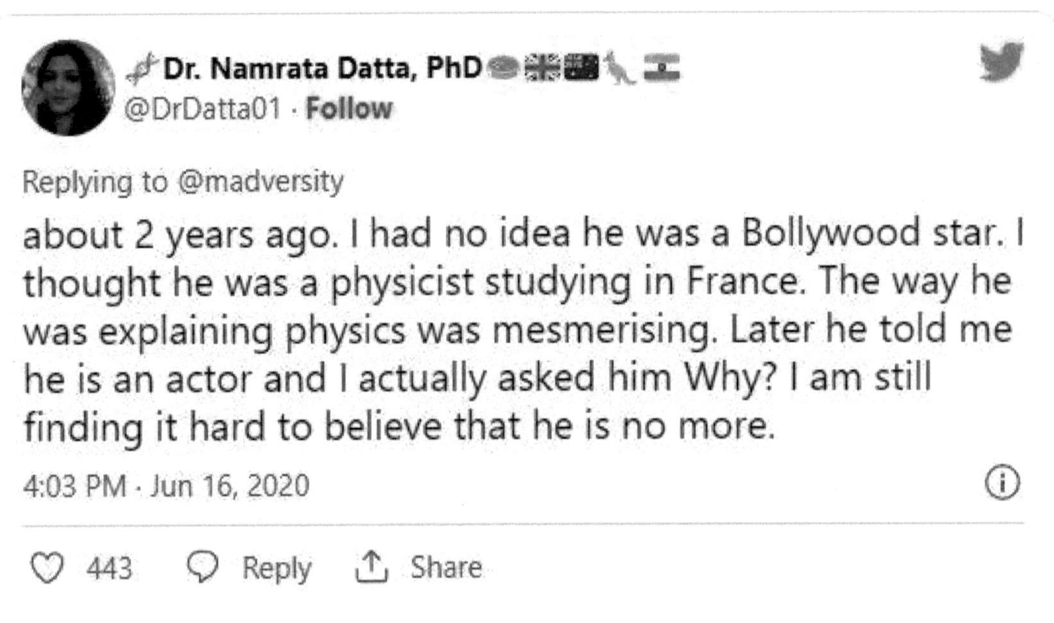

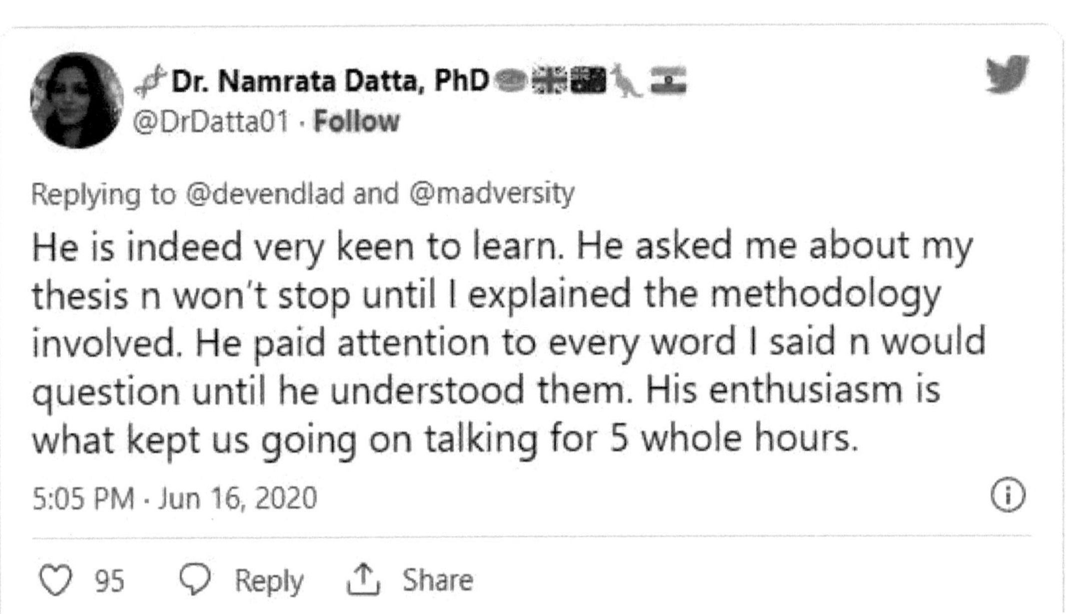

Sushant's entire Instagram is filled posts related to cosmos and its understandings. He was also the one who was very fascinated by space and astronomy. Once he was also seen being engrossed in solving a complex Physics equation which showed his passion for science.

Sushant used to keep one telescope at his home for him to see Jupiter's moon and Saturn's rings. On his walls at home he had NASA photos and spacecraft miniatures. He also used to read the books of the great writers like Richard Dawkins and Yuval Noah Harari, and his this knowledge beyond his field of acting, dance and movies was clearly seen in his speeches and interviews.

Whenever in one's life one feel stressed, he or she own her own way tries to keep the stress away, like some go for watching movies, some go outside in an open area to feel fresh while some love talk with dear ones at this situation. Sushant also talked about his stress management where he told that when he was in stress he used to solve the Math equations to keep him calm.

Sushant used to consider himself as a workaholic and he also never slept so much. In one interview he said that he slept only for 3 hours and spent most of the time in reading books.

Beyond this Sushant was also a budding entrepreneur. He loved technology. His loved for Science and Technology excited him to co-found three companies where he also played the role of director in these companies. One of his company dealt with technologies like artificial intelligence (AI), virtual reality (VR) where as his another company worked in the field of computer sciences. His startup or company was a non-profit organization which focused on health and social work.

His first company Innsai Ventures was established in May, 2018. The name, Innsai is the Icelandic word for intuition. This company works in multiple sectors such as movies, health and wellness, education, incubation, VR, AR and intellectual property. It was conceptualized as a venture to maximize the potential of technological innovations and distribute its benefits among wider population. The company has paid up capital of Rs 1 lakh. Apart from Sushant, the board of the company has co-founders Varun Mathur and Saurabh Mishra.

His second company Vividrage Rhealityx was founded in September, 2019, a year after founding Innsai Ventures. According to company's corporate filings, its business is related to exponential technology along with Mixed Reality, Artificial Intelligence and experiential technology in India and around the world. Sushant had deposited over Rs 1 lakh in the company as paid up capital. The company is headquartered in Mumbai and registered with the Registrar of Companies, Mumbai.

Sushant was also part of Front India for World Foundation, a non-profit started earlier this year. The organization was incorporated on January 6, 2020. According to the memorandum of association filed by the late actor, this organization intended to work on eradication of hunger, poverty and malnutrition, and promote healthcare, including preventive health care and sanitation. Showik, Sushant's colleague from Vividrage Rhealityx board, is also a part of the Front India for World Foundation board.

So this proves that Sushant was really a brilliant and unique personality. Not only he was a talented actor and dancer, he was also brilliant and interested in beyond dance, acting and films. He was eagerly and fascinatedly interested in Physics, Space, Science and Technology and astrophysics and even from a successful actor to a visionary entrepreneur. It's not easy to learn and achieve various different things beyond your existing field. But Sushant proved this that it's not necessary that you should stay stuck to only your existing filed, it's possible to be the person even beyond your existing field by learning various new things and applying them to make you more satisfied and different from others.

SIX

GENEROUS AND HUMBLE MAN

As seen Sushant was really talented personality and had interests and knowledge beyond his acting career, also he was also an entrepreneur. But talking about this man, he was even more than that.....He was also philanthropic and generous person. He was really generous with his wealth.

In 2018, there was a severe flood in Kerala. So back in 2018, Sushant showed his generosity, this generous person donated Rs one crore to help Keralites who were trapped in severe and worst floods.

He donated the money to the Kerala CM's relief fund after when his fan had expressed his desire to support and help the Kerala's flood relief efforts. "Sushant Singh Rajput, I don't have money but I want to donate for flood. How can I donate? Please tell me" he wrote this to Sushant by tagging him.

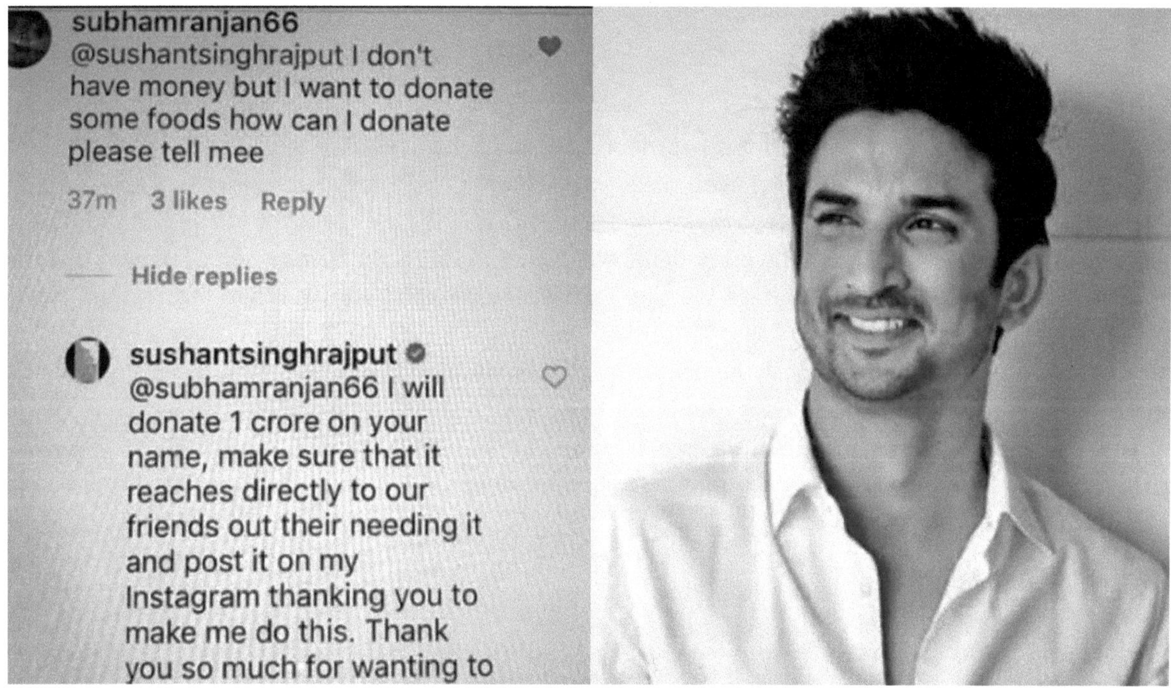

Sushant in his tweet wrote "As promised my friend, @subhamranjan66, what you wanted to do has been done. You made me do this, so be extremely proud of yourself. You delivered exactly when it was needed. Lots and lots of love. FLY. Cheers!"

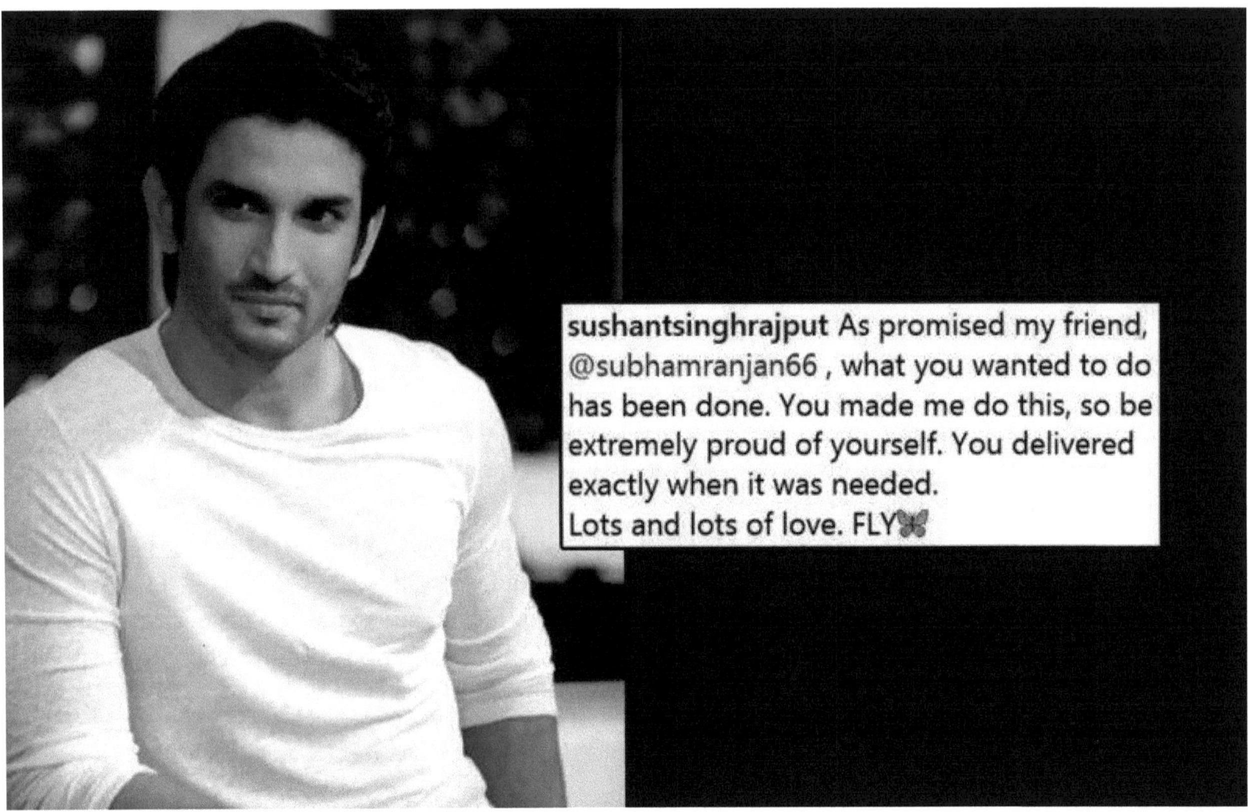

Sushant was very quick to answer and promised tom make the payments on his behalf and posted a screenshot of his contribution by adding the hashtag #MyKerala.

Kerala CM Pinarayi Vijayan expressed shock over the actor's death and tweeted "We are deeply saddened to hear of the death of Sushant Singh Rajput. His early demise is a great loss to the Indian Film industry. Our heartfelt condolences to his family, friends & supporters. We take a moment to remember his support during the time of Kerala floods."

Apart from this, Sushant also generously helped the people of Nagaland, who were also affected by floods, in the same year 2018. Here also he had donated a sum of Rs 1.25 crore to the Chief Minister's Relief Fund. Neiphiu Rio, Chief Minister of Nagaland thanked Sushant in a tweet. He wrote ""I thank Sushant Singh Rajput for standing with Nagaland. He personally handed over a cheque of Rs.1.25 crore towards CM Relief Fund. I am grateful to him and everyone who has come in support of our state."

I thank Sushant Singh Rajput @itsSSR for standing with #Nagaland. He personally handed over a cheque of Rs.1.25 crore towards CM Relief Fund. I am grateful to him and everyone who has come in support of our state #NagalandFloods #DonateForNagaland

Why? At that neither his any of the film's promotion was going, in fact Kerala and Nagaland were also not his target audience, but still yet he wanted to help the people...And that's what made him special. He understood the pain of common people.

Today, after the actor's untimely demise, the Nagaland CM wrote "Shocked & saddened to hear about the untimely demise of Sushant Singh Rajput. He personally handed over a cheque to me when Nagaland was affected by floods & landslides in 2018. His love & generous contribution to the people of Nagaland will always be remembered. May his soul RIP."

Sushant was also known for helping individuals in need. Once a Twitter user wrote to him asking for help with regard to his father's cancer treatment and the actor replied "Please tell me what I could do. Prayers for the father."

Sushant once highlighted the importance of education in an interview and said, "My mother always taught me that we educate our children not to become a doctor or engineer, but the impact of basic education reflects on their thought process and decision making. So even if you are getting into a creative profession like acting, your basic education will open your mind enough to think analytically."

Converting his beliefs into actions, the actor along with his team worked out an idea where they would conduct a merit test in some of the selected schools and would provide free education for a year for all the students who pass the test. The students will have to take the test each year to secure free education. This way the students are encouraged to study and do not take the opportunity for granted.

Apart from these initiatives, the actor was generally kind to his fans. He often conversed with them and followed them back on social media to make them happy.

There's one more incidence of his humbleness, once when other celebrities were ignoring and denying brushing off some balloon sellers who wanted wanted to shoot a photo with them, on the same hand when they wanted to take a photo with

Sushant he didn't ignored them, he didn't denied them and he didn't brushed them off indeed he shook hands with them and even treated them with respect.

We notice that when people achieve big things and reach at a level of big success in life they start thinking that other people are beneath them. But Sushant was different and special. And this why when we came to know that Sushant is no more we were shocked.

Really salute to you to Sushant....for your true generosity for understanding the pain of the common people and helping them...Salute to you man for humbleness for not considering anyone beneath you and considering every one equally and treating everyone equally.

"Stars always shine no matter where they are."

SEVEN
Words of Sushant

1.

"Do what you love":

"I have started from nothing, absolutely nothing. It's not even zero. It's like minus because I was doing something else. There was a momentum to become an engineer and suddenly I discovered was this thing that I really like and I start doing it. But at the same time, as a kid, I also had many dreams, like common dreams. I'll buy my own house and I'll buy a luxury car. So these things were there. And now when I started following my dream in the sense of changing my career, I started earning money to an extent that I could actually afford all these things.

What happened that while I was doing my work, I also was realizing this fact that everything that I stayed with for so many years, for 20 years of my life, thinking that one day I'll get this and then I'll arrive, I'll be successful. Those things just stayed with me for a few days and I very quickly got used to owning those things. And there was no excitement left. So I was like, oh, this is not the way to go. But then the only way to go is to be myopic, so another goal, another goal. But it doesn't give you anything. The entire process will bore you until unless you get something and it will just hit you for like few days and then again. So it's like 95% of boredom and 5% of excitement. But if you do something every day that excites you, you will get all those things.

You'll get the spikes in between, but at the same time you're enjoying the entire process, failures. It's extremely important.

I think I would value a massive failure more than a mediocre success. But having said that, that's not my intent why I'll do something. But the most important thing is that the whole knowledge structure of education in our schools or anything, we are taught to be so careful. We are taught or do not fail. You have to succeed.

That's fine. You want to succeed, you please succeed. But being careful is the problem. You need to learn how not to be careful.

You need to try different things. Only then once, in like 100 times or 200times, you hit on something that's completely fresh. And that's going to change everything for everybody. So it's extremely important to fail, because without failure you cannot get something new or fresh. You'll be a very good reputation of something else, if that makes you happy."

2. *"I perform better when I don't know that there is plan B":*

"I started off as a being this very shy and introverted kid. Because I was the youngest in the family very pampered. I didn't know how to deal with the people when I used to step out. So any sort of acknowledgment meant a lot. Money was always a differentiator in my life. So money and any sort of acknowledgement were two big differentiators.

And I was told that if you get these two, you will be successful. And I cleared all these Engineering Entrance Exams, and I was studying, and I was just aware of what was happening. And I felt that, okay, this is not something, it's not giving me that high because it's boring.

I was told that choose one thing. And they asked me, my parents and mine everybody who love me. They said that you need to be an engineer. I have four sisters, so they were asked to be doctors. I was asked to be an engineer. And if you were good at what we were doing, we were expected to sit for civil services....And that was the thing.

After clearing such a top Engineering Entrance Exams, when I went to that college, I found that there were no girls. And I was like, I felt cheated, I was like, okay, this is not what it is, because they told me that work hard, be an engineer, and marry a nice girl, and that's what will happen.....But there were no girls in my college.

Somebody told me that, why don't you join dance school? And I went there. But something very interesting happened, while I was performing for the first time, I recognized this want of me, that I really want to be, or probably wanting to be understood...And that was the starting point. Shiamak asked me to do the theater.

Somebody said, that, okay, you can't actually make somebody an actor, but you can train an actor. So I was like, what if I am not an actor? So I went to Barry John and I was there for three, four months when we got a certificate. And I got a B grade and everybody else got C. So that's when I got to realize, okay, this is something I really can do. Also, because, I could hide behind all these interesting characters. You know, I could hide behind all these interesting characters. I could say things that I really want to say. But at the same time, I can tell people that, oh, this is not me, this is the character.

I was like okay, this is something that I really want to do, even if I don't get paid for it, I still do it.

So just being aware of the process, and I just telling myself that if I can be top 1% in something which I probable don't like, now I've identified something that I do like, and I don't care what people think of me. It doesn't feel like hard work. I want to take risks. There's nothing else but to perseverance is the thing, because that's the only thing that I want to do. So all these things were at place and identifying that, I was like, okay, this is something I like.

I can very well be in the top 1% of this. And just being clear about my awareness, I dropped out.

There are two things to it. Number one was, how did I convince myself into dropping out of a very prestigious engineering college... Into something which is very dicey...And number two, what I found while doing it...So number one was that if I could be in top 1% is something that I don't like, I can be very be in top 1%, which I absolutely like. And I promised myself a fancy house, fancy car. So I was like, okay, this is what you'll get and drop out. And just six to eight months away from getting my self-degree....I dropped out...Because I thought that it will be a better state to be in if I don't have a plan B.......Because I won't be thinking that if nothing happens, I'll go back to this. I perform better when I don't know that there is plan B."

Life Inspiring quotes of Sushant:

1. "I have been overshadowed for the first 25 years of my life when I was nobody to the world. But I was a superstar in my head!"
2. "For me the opposite of happiness is not sadness, but boredom."

1. "Just doing good work matters to me. I might be doing TV, theatre or movies or, for that matter, open a canteen in a film city or work on my short films. I don't have the fear of failure."
2. "I won't lie and say that I'm not seduced by fame and money. But what has kept me going is the excitement of finding a character and living him."
3. "I want to fail, but it should not be a mediocre failure. It should be massive. *Ek ehsaas karne ke liye* it is important to fail badly and destroy me as an individual. At the same time, I don't want mediocre success either."

- Quotes by Legendary Mr. Sushant Singh Rajput

EIGHT

14TH JUNE........

It was 14th June, it was complete lockdown. I had went with my uncle for some work. We were busy in our work till afternoon 12 PM and returned back at home till 1:00 clock back to home. As usual my uncle has the habit of watching the news after doing or finishing with his work for a sort of break. So he switched on the television for watching the news. He put on the News Channel on TV....and what I heard and what my uncle heard from the news was shocking.......

Just few 2 or 3 days before 14th June 2020 I had watched 'MS Dhoni: The Untold Story' again I had also seen this movie in the movie theatre when it was first released in November 2016 (after watching this film in theatre to be honest I really became a big fan of Sushant and now also I'm), I also watched it again on TV because I really loved that film (now also I watch it for inspiration) because the way Sushant had gone into the character of Dhoni was really stunning, he played and practiced cricket for playing the role this movie so mostly Sushant inspires me the most from this movie. I watched it again in June 2020 in lockdown, few days before 14th June......

And it was 14th June 1:00 or 1:30 PM, my uncle and I heard a very shocking and heartbreaking news.......Sushant Sir was no more in this world.....I was stunned and shocked at that time....no words to say....how, why, when, what, where...I was in complete dilemmatic situation....because I was really a big fan of this man for his brilliantness, intelligence, hard work, perseverance, risk taking attitude, dedication.....and hearing this that this great personality was no more.....

Now also I really miss Sushant. We all really miss Sushant not because he was a successful actor, we miss him because he was more than a successful actor.....he was generous, he was philantrophic, he was humble and down to earth man, he was brilliant, he was intelligent, he was a deep thinker...and many more. After hearing that Sushant was no more we were really shocked. Now also we miss him too much...

"Sushant Singh Rajput, you are missed" By - Subhash K Jha:

Sushant too was a fighter. A fierce fighter. He worked on his own term. "I work entirely for my job satisfaction. Otherwise, I could have made money in any other profession. I am here to make a difference, firstly to myself. When I look back on my body of work I want to feel a sense of pride. Whether it is *Kai Po Che, Byomkesh Bakshi, Dhoni, Kedarnath* or *Sonchiriya*, I am happy and proud to be associated with these films. I am not in this for the money or the fame. I don't care about money, as long as I have enough to look after my basic needs and the needs of family and team. I am not intimidated by anyone. Nor will be bullied into doing any film that I don't want to do. My workspace and my private space is non- negotiable. I feel there is an appreciation for all the hard work being put in my films. Maybe in my case, it doesn't show in box office figures. But as long as I've the freedom and power to do the kind of films I want to I am in a comfortable place."

This was the bravest actor of his generation who never played it safe. Sushant said no to Sanjay Leela Bhansali's *Goliyon Ki Raasleela Ram Leela*: he was busy training for Shekhar Kapur's *Paani* which Aditya Chopra's Yash Raj Films was to produce. An ambitious retelling of *Romeo & Juliet* set in the future when water was the battering ram that determined your status in society, the preparation and workshops for *Paani* took two years of Sushant's precious all-too-brief life.

Would he have avoided wasting those two years if he knew he had so little time to live? I think he wouldn't have.

Once I asked him if he regretted losing out on so many plum assignments for *Paani*, Sushant's reply was revealing. "Not at all. I would do it again, even if I was told at the beginning that the film would not be made. In those two years, I learnt so much from Shekhar Sir. He is an entire institution of filmmaking. Just being with him was a learning experience."

I didn't agree with Sushant. Especially now when I look back, I wonder why Sushant chose to lose those two years: he had so little time. He could have done at least two more films during the *Paani* break.

Sushant did just ten full-length feature films during his lifetime. Of these Abhishek Choubey's *Sonchiriya* was his proudest achievement. Shooting for his outlaw's role in *Sonchiriya* Sushant spent days and weeks preparing himself, staying unwashed, unfed, unattended. "My character wants to surrender to the law. I surrendered to the law of self-discipline that I've made for my job. I had to capture the core of humanity in my character. That said, success or failure is not something I understand."

I still have Sushant's last WhatsApp message to me. I have read it many times over since his death. It says, "Sir, I remember that I have what all I want already, so I don't offer any negotiation with my peace or smiles in any ones presence or absence. And we know that it could only get better from here."

Sadly, it didn't get better from there. The message sent on 27 March 2019 was the last I heard from Sushant. One year three months later, Sushant was no more. In the interim, I made many attempts to reach him. His number was unreachable. None of his friends knew where he was.

Words, as they say, fail to convey the ridiculousness of the situation.

By - Subhash K Jha

(Subhash K Jha is a Patna-based film critic who has been writing about Bollywood for long enough to know the industry inside out.)

NINE

LAST FILM 'DIL BECHARA'...

'Dil Bechara' is such a film which represents love, hope and loss all such emotions in a very great way. After passing of Sushant this film keeps a very sentimental value for all of us. When I watched this film I became really so much emotional indeed I cried because the this movie say so much about LIFE and the man, to whom I was seeing on the screen is no more... this also made me feel emotional. I would recommend to you friends to watch this film. Because it's really amazing film which says so much about LIFE....

1.

Keep Smiling:

Sushant's character in this film lights up every situation through his humor. By this we come to know that in life if we add humor then the life becomes little better. In this film Sushant's character Manny also have several problems in his life it's because, because of cancer he had lost his one leg...but still yet, despite of this Manny is always seen smiling. Usually if such incident happens with someone else then his or her life becomes very difficult...but through Manny's character we are shown the LIFE in different perspective. Kizie the girl and main lead female role in this film is annoyed and tired with her daily routine...but when Manny enters in her life, her life gets transformed in a new life.

Manny always keep laughing on any matter and also makes other smile and laugh due to which Kizie also start living happily.

In same way in our life too....when we are in any of the difficult phase then sometimes we should SMILE because we don't know when will the problems go, but if we SMILE then at least our day will be good and even the people around you by getting attracted to your this energy become happy.

2. Live your Life at the Fullest:

In this film many character believes in living the life at fullest. When Manny feels to dance then before coming of his turn he starts dancing in front of the whole college. Rather than this he also does acting in his friend's film where he pays a kind of tribute to his idol Rajnikanth. These all things try to depict Manny's philosophy that how he believes in living his each and every day at the fullest.

We too in our life when become busy at something, we stop thinking about our dreams or maybe we think about completing those dreams in future....but as we all know that in future we are not able to remove time for our dreams....similarly Kizie had also stopped thinking about her dreams because she thinks that her life is situated in just home and hospital...But when Manny comes in her life Kizie starts completing her wish list. They often go to Paris. So whatever dreams or wish list or wishes you have starting acting and working for them as early as possible because when you think about completing any dream behind this many small-small dreams also start getting completed.

3. Never lose Hope:

IN movie 'Dil Bechara' HOPE plays very important role. Manny brings new hopein Kizie's life, and when afterwards Manny is in difficult situation Kizie become a very big hope for Manny. IN our life several such moments come where we leave our hope...at such situation we should have a little hope that further life will not remain like this. Rather than this if we are very close to someone we should always give hope to that person in difficult times because just by your hope or staying with that person in such times, may the things become better. In this film we see the same situation where very character gives hope to each other.

Along with Kizie Manny is also seen giving hope to his friend Jagdish and also helps in completing his feelings. After this when Manny himself is in difficult situation i.e. he starts suffering from cancer, rather than calling doctor he prefers to call Kizie, which clearly shows that Manny sees Kizie as his big hope.

4. Everyone is fighting their own battles:

In our life whatever we do, whatever we are doing, but in our life there are some problems present, but don't this thing negatively because it's the human nature that we always keep fighting for the difficult problems.

In this film each character is fighting with his own problems whether it's Kizie suffering from her illness or whether her parents struggling to take care of her or whether Manny's personal problems. These scenes show us that each one is dealing with his own difficulties and rather than increasing their difficulties we should be with them, support them.

5. Life is Unpredictable and Incomplete:

Many a times it happens that in life few things happen suddenly that we are not able to understand how to deal with that situation. Manny's character lived his character very happily but a situation comes where his cancer comes back and he's not able to deal with his life' situation. This situation makes us understand that life is really unpredictable and further what will happen we don't know.

This why is this film Manny says this golden line ***"Janam kab lena hai aur marna kab hai woh hum decide nahi kar sakte, par kaise jeena hai who hum decide kar sakte hain."***

TEN

Sushant was no doubt a very great personality who earned people's love and respect when he was alive and continues to do so even after his death. Sushant's most positive trait was winning people over with love and respected for them i.e. he knew how to wing people's heart. By applying his personality traits and life lessons we can also change our life too by becoming not a successful human but being a good human....

Is Money Everthing?

People often think that they achieve and earn respect when they are wealthy and rich. Wealth does not mean money, wealth has different meanings for different people. Most of the people's tendency is that once they become rich, once they have handsome net worth then they automatically get respect which they deserve for being RICH. But once Henry Ford said, if you want respect, then you should focus on three things; your skillset, your life experiences and most importantly your knowledge.....

And Sushant honestly believed in these three things. Let's see his experiences on these thing by himself.

1. Sushant, the great reader and learner

"So what happens is that when you read a lot, those are the writers that think in your brain for the time when you're reading. So, it's like ranting your brain for that writer to think till the time you are reading a book. So, if you read multiple books on a particular subject, so you have multiple point of views on the same thing. So, a really a good place to be and everyone should read and read a lot.

And then there is thing that we understand now is that the more you learn, the less time it takes to learn more.

Generally we think that we are left with so much time and we are so busy in our life and there are so many years left....how many things can we learn? What will happen? ...no it's that, the more you learn, the lesser it will take to learn more. And that's a very key thing to understand. So you will start learning many things, things that you will try for the first time, will be 5% easier for you than anybody else."

- By Sushant....

2. Limitless person:

"The moment you pinpoint your limits, you instantly become limitless, which is a very important thing to understand, I guess.

I can say that if you have philosophical bent of mind, you will end earning a lot of money. So, this is a trend of exponential technology....like that the merger of biotech and infotech is one, 3D printing is second, AI is third and Virtual Reality.

Curiosity, my heart and brain are jittering which never leaves me...."

And this is the real wealth which Sushant had and he earned real respect because of this wealth.

Sushant won people's heart and respect through his brain. But Sushant also won people's heart through his behavior and body language.

Sushant himself said that he was an introvert, he was a kid inside. Take for example of alpha male Bollywood celebrities...how did they present themselves in an interview? Through a loud and strong body language, loud voice. But if you you check any of Sushant's interview, he would talk to his hosts very calmly and very sweetly. And what would he talk about? He talked not just about his films, not just about his career, but he also talked Artificial Intelligence, Physics, future, of business....and he would explain all these concepts very sweetly and with a sweet and positive smile on his face.

The way the kid is excited and curious to know things, similarly Sushant was also excited and curious to know these big subjects. HE had so much of knowledge, so much of experiences...but he always presented himself just like any curious kid who excited discover the new things. He would make eye contact and explain concepts happily. When he had any kind of deep thought then he would start looking down and break contact, he would then think it through and explain something to host in a very good way....as if he genuinely wanted to share his knowledge with people. This called as Multi-Dimensional vibe which means the ability to talk like a senior and act like a junior. People are aware that you're

intelligent, you're senior, you have knowledge and experiences but people also know that this person is like a friend to them...and this is how Sushant won the hearts of many people. Which is why, people love him so dearly despite he is not in this world. He was knowledgeable and as well as sweet.

But along with this, Sushant also had a kind of magnet in his brain, a thing that drew people towards him and found him attractive because of that........

"Understand it this that if I want every individual to rich, successful and famous in their life only to understand that it had nothing.

The closest synonym to happiness and excitement which only occurs when you do something that you love.

Study methods in engineering are a way of thinking which we consider to be very amazing cognitive tool. You can apply that thought process anywhere, even in Bollywood and anything can happen "

And that thing which can be realized from his above said words is happiness and excitement. We often meet people who are unforgettable, and they are so happy from inside that we can't keep their happiness away from them. We keep their happiness inside our heart. We remember people for their happiness. So you should focus on happiness, if you want to be someone memorable. So focus on your happiness.

Sushant would always talk about the wealth driven games.....

"We have tried to educate people about education through Chhichhore. Similarly there things in our heart that we would keep expressing through films. And if someone wants to prove that they can work, so for that I have opened my companies. In that, we work on sustainable energy and AI. Ultimately, keep dreaming and living....."

From opening up businesses, sharing knowledge, winning over people. Internally, Sushant was a very happy man. The secret to his happiness was his excitement to feel excited, motivated and enthusiastic in everything he did....and the secret to that excitement was his curiosity to understand something in so depth that we can explain that to others clearly.

Someone asked him that when you acted in theater or on TV, did you feel that you want to get into films? To this this is what Sushant replied.....

"Something that has gone right for me is, I don't differentiate the medium. I don't care if it is a TV camera, film camera or I am performing on stage. Ultimately, we have to forget all that and punctuate presence over productivity, as I said. So this process of thinking that from theater to TV to OTT film is a graduation, this I feel is very limited mindset and this does not happen. This is not a concept for an artist, art is the most important for them......"

More things to learn from Sushant:

1. **"Don't do it for fame or money:** Ask yourself why you want to do it. I really, absolutely love what I do. If your answer is fame or money, it is not going to work. I come from a middle-class family and there are things I couldn't afford earlier. I thought it is the money that is keeping me from being happy, but that is not the case. In this profession, if you make it to a certain level, you will have money and fame. But if that is your motivation, then what will you do next? You can't get more famous after a point and then it becomes a flat graph. It will then fail to make you happy."

2. **"Enjoy the journey:** Don't concentrate on 'how to get there', instead enjoy the getting there. Realise where you are today and enjoy that. I don't believe in cause and effect. I think whatever happens, happens first and then we manufacture the cause to justify it. I didn't plan my career and I don't think that now that I have a sea-facing house in Bandra, I am in a more secure position than I was in the 1 RK apartment. There are too many variables in the working. I don't extend my time to future: it is the present, the now, that I am enjoying."

3. **"Don't use luck as an excuse:** People often ask why after Shah Rukh Khan, I am the only actor who could successfully make the transition from television to movies. Let me recount an incident from the sports history. In 1954, Roger Bannister was the first man ever to run a mile in less than four minutes, till then it was an unheard of feat. But the very next year 27 other people achieved the same feat. This was because they thought that if he can do it, so can we. But here, most people think that oh this guy just got lucky, and they don't put in the effort. Luck is a factor, definitely, but don't make it your excuse."

So these are things that you can learn from Sushant. He earned respect through his reading and knowledge. He earned respect through his politeness or humility. And why do we remember him? Because he was a wealth driven man who had correct mentality, he carried a lot of curiosity in his heart. This person gave so much positivity to the world. Learn from the great personalities like Sushant Singh Rajput.

Sushant left this world with inspiration, motivation, knowledge...he left with the correct mentality and guidance.

WE ALL LOVE YOU SUSHANT.....

Sushant Singh Rajput

(January 21, 1986 – June 14, 2020)

Printed by Libri Plureos GmbH in Hamburg,
Germany